Contents

Dedication

To my stepmother, the woman who raised me, loved me, and never left me.

"Your love was my foundation. Your strength became my guide. Even in your absence, your presence remains in every step I take, in every lesson I pass down, in every moment I strive to be the man you always believed I could be."

This book is for you.

"Your love never left me. And it never will."

Rest In Peace
Gloristine "MA" Sherrod
June 28, 1945 - January 21, 2010

The Night Before the Wedding

A Restless Night Filled with Memories

The night before my wedding should have been filled with excitement. Maybe a little nervousness, but mostly joy. But as I sat alone in my hotel room, staring out at the city lights, a wave of emotion crept over me like an unshakable shadow.

I had made it. I had found love, built a life, and tomorrow, I would stand at the altar, vowing forever to the woman I loved.

But no matter how much I tried to focus on the happiness of the moment, something in me felt... incomplete. Because she wasn't here. My stepmother. The woman who raised me, protected me, guided me. The woman who had poured all her love into me, making sure I never went without. The woman who had been both a mother and a father, who had given everything she had to ensure I was loved, safe, and prepared for the world.

I should have been waking up to a phone call from her. "Boy, you up yet? I know you ain't slept a wink!"

I should have been walking into the church and seeing her sitting proudly in the front row, beaming at me, maybe wiping a tear away. I should have been hearing her fuss over me, making sure my suit was right, making sure my shoes were shining, making sure I wasn't "looking any kind of way."

But she wasn't here. And that realization broke something inside me.

I clenched my hands into fists against my knees as the silence in the room grew unbearable. The only sound was the faint hum of the air conditioner and the distant cars outside. The night felt too quiet, too still.

Then, before I could stop myself, the words slipped out, raw and broken: "I wish you were here. You would be so proud of me." The moment the words left my lips, the air in the room felt different. As if something—someone—was listening.

Memories Flooding In

I squeezed my eyes shut, and suddenly, I wasn't in my hotel room anymore. I was a little boy again, standing in the doorway of our home, watching her iron my clothes.

She always made sure I looked sharp, pressing my shirts perfectly, smoothing out every wrinkle. She'd look me over, nodding in approval, and say, "Now you look like somebody."

She took pride in the way I carried myself, in the way I presented myself to the world. "Ain't no son of mine walking around looking any kind of way," she'd say, adjusting my collar, making sure my socks weren't twisted.

And now, here I was, the night before one of the biggest moments of my life... and she wasn't here to make sure everything was just right.

I opened my eyes and glanced at my wedding suit hanging neatly in the closet. She would have loved it. She would have fussed over the details, straightened my tie a hundred times, wiped imaginary lint off my shoulders, and told me to stand tall.

And she would have looked at my bride—the woman I had chosen—and I know she would have smiled. She would have been proud. But she wasn't here. And that realization crushed me.

The Breakdown

The tears started slow at first, burning at the edges of my eyes, threatening to spill. I clenched my jaw, trying to fight them back, trying to remind myself that I was a grown man now. That this wasn't the time to fall apart.

But grief doesn't listen to reason. My shoulders shook as the dam broke. Tears slipped down my face, and soon, the quiet weeping turned into full, heaving sobs. I wasn't just crying for tomorrow. I was crying for every moment she had missed. Every time I had needed her voice, her touch, her presence. Every milestone she hadn't been there to witness. The first time I got my own place. The first time I got a real job. The nights I stayed up late, wishing I could call her for advice, but knowing there would be no answer.

I wasn't just crying for the wedding. I was crying for all the days before it. For all the times I had been strong. For all the times I had swallowed my pain and kept moving forward. For all the years I had convinced myself that I was okay.

And then, suddenly, the crying slowed. The weight in my chest remained, but something else settled beside it. A warmth. A presence.

I wasn't sure if it was just a memory, or if maybe, just maybe, she was there in some way I couldn't fully understand. But deep inside, I knew. She was proud.

The Church: Feeling Her Presence

The next morning, when I walked into the church, my heart clenched. The scent of old wooden pews mixed with the fresh flowers from the wedding decorations. The sunlight streamed through the stained-glass windows, casting colors across the floor.

I closed my eyes for a moment and just felt it. She was here. I didn't know how I knew—I just did.

Maybe it was the church itself—her favorite place, the space where she had always found comfort. Maybe it was the prayers that had been spoken in this building, the songs that had been sung, the echoes of faith that she had carried so deeply within her. But as I stood at the front of the church, waiting for my bride, I felt an overwhelming sense of peace. She wasn't in the front row. But she was here.

Carrying Her With Me

As I stood at the altar, waiting for my bride to walk down the aisle, I realized something. Love doesn't leave. It changes. It shifts. It moves in ways we don't always understand. But it never truly disappears.

My stepmother's love was still here. It was in the way I carried myself. It was in the way I had chosen a woman who truly loved me. It was in the church walls, in the memories, in the very air I breathed.

And as my bride finally stepped through the doors, as she walked toward me with love in her eyes, I whispered one last thought in my mind. *"I hope you see me, Mama. I hope you see what I've built, what I've become. I hope you know that everything you poured into me... it wasn't in vain."*

And for the first time since the night before, I felt something other than grief.

I felt her love. I felt her presence. And I knew, deep in my heart...

She was walking with me.

The Wedding Day

JOY AND HEARTBREAK

Waking Up to a Heavy Heart

The morning of my wedding should have felt different. I should have woken up with excitement, with nerves about seeing my bride, with nothing but joy in my heart. But instead, I woke up to an empty room, the echoes of last night's tears still lingering on my face.

I stared at the ceiling, my chest feeling hollow. The weight from the night before hadn't lifted—it had only settled deeper.

Today was supposed to be the happiest day of my life. And yet, something inside me still ached. Because she wasn't here.

I rolled over, looking at my phone, half-expecting to see a text from her. But there was nothing.

No *"I'm proud of you, baby."* No *"You better not cry in front of that woman."* Nothing.

I shut my eyes, swallowing the pain.

I had to be strong today. I had to be present. But damn...

It was hard.

Getting Dressed: Feeling Her Absence

I moved through the motions of getting ready like I was on autopilot. Shower. Shave. Suit.

Each step felt mechanical, each movement careful and precise.

But when I finally looked at myself in the mirror, fully dressed, I froze.

My stepmother should have been here. She should have been standing behind me, straightening my collar, making sure my suit was perfect. She should have been running her hands over my shoulders, checking for lint that wasn't even there.

She should have been nagging me, *"Boy, don't you go out there looking wrinkled. You know better."*

Instead, it was just me. Alone.

I adjusted my tie, trying to imagine what she would say if she could see me now.

"You look good, baby. Just like I knew you would."

I let out a slow breath. I had to keep moving. Because today, no matter how much it hurt...

I had to make her proud.

Walking into the Church: Feeling Her Presence

The moment I stepped into the church, something shifted. The scent of polished wood and fresh flowers filled the air, the light from the stained-glass windows casting colors across the floor. The hum of quiet conversations surrounded me, guests settling into their seats.

But beyond all of that, I felt *her*. It was a warmth, a presence I couldn't explain. Maybe it was the memories of all the Sundays we had spent in church together. Maybe it was the way the choir hummed softly in the background, a sound so familiar it almost brought me to my knees.

Or maybe...

Maybe she really was here. Watching. Smiling. Proud.

I let out a slow breath, standing tall.

"You got this, baby." For a brief moment, I almost believed I had heard her voice.

The Pain of an Empty Seat

Then, my eyes landed on the front row. My stepsisters were sitting there, two of them dressed in their finest, smiling softly as they looked toward me.

But there was an empty seat. The third stepsister—the one who should have been there—was missing.

I had invited her. She had been part of my life for as long as I could remember. And yet, she hadn't come.

A dull ache settled in my chest. Had she chosen not to be here? Was it too hard for her? Did she not care?

I clenched my jaw, forcing myself to look away. I couldn't focus on that right now. Today wasn't about who wasn't here. It was about who was. And as painful as it was, I had to push forward.

The Moment My Bride Walked In

Then, the music started. I turned my head. And there she was.

My bride.

She was breathtaking, a vision in white, her eyes locked onto mine. And in that moment, the ache in my chest loosened. Because even though today carried grief, it also carried love. And this woman—the one walking toward me—was the love I had been waiting for.

I felt my throat tighten. Not from sadness. But from the overwhelming realization that, despite everything... I had found happiness. I had found a future. And I had found a love that my stepmother would have approved of.

"Mama, I hope you see this. I hope you see her." Because I knew—deep in my heart—she would have loved my bride. She would have pulled me aside and said, *"Now that's the kind of woman you build a life with."*

I swallowed hard, blinking back the emotion as my bride finally reached me. I took her hands in mine. And for the first time that day, I felt... okay.

The Vows: Holding Back Tears

As I stood there, looking into the eyes of the woman I loved, I thought about all the moments that had led me here. The struggles. The losses. The lessons. The love.

I took a deep breath, gripping my bride's hands a little tighter.

"I promise to love you, to honor you, to stand beside you in all that life brings..." My voice wavered slightly, and I had to pause. Because at that moment, I felt something else. That warmth again. That presence. That feeling that I wasn't standing here alone.

She was here. Watching. Smiling. Holding me up in a way that only she could.

And as I finished my vows, I knew...

She had never really left me.

Final Reflection: Carrying Love and Loss Together

Love and loss exist together. You can't have one without the other.

And standing there, at the altar, I realized... My stepmother's love had carried me here. Every lesson. Every sacrifice. Every word of wisdom.

She had shaped me into the man I was.

And even though she wasn't physically here, I felt her. I carried her with me. In my heart. In my vows. In the way I loved my wife.

Her love was still alive.

And as I leaned in to kiss my bride, I whispered a final thought in my mind. *"Mama, I did it."*

And for the first time all day...

I felt at peace.

Childhood

BEING HER ONLY SON

A Love Like No Other

From the moment I could remember, my stepmother's love surrounded me like a shield.

I wasn't just a child in her home—I was her son. Her pride. Her greatest responsibility.

She had three daughters, all of them twenty years older than me, but I was the baby. And I wasn't just raised by her—I was her world.

She never dated. Never brought men around. Never let anything or anyone distract her from raising me the way she wanted to.

"Ain't nobody gonna raise my son but me." She said it with a certainty that made it clear—she had chosen this life. She didn't just love me; she protected me.

Everywhere she went, I was right by her side. She never let me out of her sight. If she went to church, I was there. If she went to the store, I was holding her hand. If she was sitting on the porch talking to a neighbor, I was on the step next to her, listening, learning.

I was hers. And no one—no one—was going to tell her how to raise her son.

The Only Boy in a House of Women

Growing up as the only boy in a house full of women was... an experience.

My stepsisters were grown women by the time I was old enough to understand the world around me. They weren't just big sisters—they were like second mothers. They helped raise me, bathed me, fed me, scolded me, spoiled me. I was their baby, too. And trust me, they let it be known.

"You know you got it good, right?" one of them would tease, pinching my cheek. I would roll my eyes and push their hands away, acting like I hated it. But deep down, I knew. I was loved.

But that didn't mean life was always easy. Because when you're the only boy in a house full of women, you're both spoiled and overprotected. I couldn't go just anywhere. I couldn't do just anything. They kept a close watch on me.

And sometimes... It felt like a cage.

Her Sacrifices: The Best for Her Son

My stepmother worked hard—real hard. She made sure I had the best clothes, always dressed me sharp, and never let me go without.

I remember shopping trips where she would take me to the department store, carefully picking out my outfits, making sure I looked like I came from something good.

"You ain't gonna walk around here looking raggedy," she'd say, shaking her head. And she meant it.

She spent what little she had to make sure I was always clean, always presentable. It didn't matter if money was tight—she found a way.

I didn't understand the sacrifices then. The nights she went without so I could have. The extra shifts she worked to afford the little luxuries she gave me. But now, as a man, I look back and see it.

She gave me everything she had.

Flashback: A Shopping Trip with Her

I still remember one particular shopping trip—one that I didn't realize would stick with me for the rest of my life. We were at the store, and I saw a pair of shoes that I had to have. They were the freshest pair I had ever seen—black with white accents, shining under the fluorescent lights like they were waiting just for me.

I ran my fingers over them, imagining how good they would look on my feet. "Mama, these the ones," I said, turning to her.

She looked at the price tag, her lips pressing together slightly. I didn't know it at the time, but now, I realize she was doing the math in her head, figuring out if she could stretch her money enough to afford them. She didn't say a word. She just nodded and took them to the register.

When we got home, I laced them up, admiring them on my feet.

"You like 'em?" she asked, smiling.

"Yeah, Mama, these the best ones yet!"

She nodded. "Good. Make sure you take care of 'em, you hear me?"

I did.

What I didn't know was that she had skipped buying something for herself that day—again.

But that's just who she was. She never said a word about what she sacrificed.

She just loved.

Her Overprotective Nature: "Ain't Nobody Gonna Hurt My Baby"

My stepmother wasn't just loving—she was protective. Overprotective, if you asked anybody else. She kept me close, always watching, always making sure I was safe. If I went outside, she was checking on me. If I was at school, she made sure the teachers knew who I belonged to. If someone even looked like they were going to mess with me, she was there—ready to handle it.

"Ain't nobody gonna hurt my baby." That was her mantra.

And she meant it.

Flashback: The Time She Checked a Teacher

One time, a teacher raised their voice at me a little too much for her liking. The next day, she was up at that school, purse in one hand, attitude in the other.

"I need to have a word with you." She didn't yell. She didn't curse. She just spoke. And when my stepmother spoke, people listened.

I don't know what she said, but after that day, that teacher treated me real nice.

That's just who she was. She didn't play about me.

Bedtime Talks and Her Words of Wisdom

At night, when the world was quiet, I would sit with her, listening to her stories, soaking in her wisdom. She had sayings—words she lived by.

"God won't bless no mess."

"Find you a good woman and not be with a mud duck."

"Ain't nobody gonna raise my son but me."

She said them all the time. But I didn't realize until later just how much those words would stick with me. She wasn't just talking. She was teaching. She was laying the foundation for the man I would become. And I didn't even know it.

The Unbreakable Bond: A Love That Shaped Me

Looking back, I realize now—her love shaped everything about me. The way I love. The way I raise my own children. The way I protect and provide.

Everything she gave me, everything she sacrificed—it wasn't for nothing. It's still in me. It's in the way I carry myself. It's in the way I build my family. It's in the way I love.

Her love wasn't just a phase of my childhood. It was the foundation of my life.

And no matter how many years pass...

I will *always* be her son.

The Last Goodbye

LOSING MY STEPMOTHER

The Last Visit: Her Final Words to Me

I didn't know it would be the last time I saw her.

If I had known, I would have stayed longer. I would have memorized the way she looked at me, the way she said my name, the way she laughed. I would have paid attention to every little detail—how she held her hands together when she spoke, the way her eyes softened when she looked at me, the rhythm of her voice when she told me the same things she had told me all my life.

"God won't bless no mess."

"Find you a good woman and not be with a mud duck."

She said it every time I visited, like it was her duty to make sure I never forgot. That day was no different. She sat in her chair, rocking slightly, her eyes studying me as if she were trying to make sure I was really okay.

"You eating good?" she asked.

"Yeah, Mama."

"You staying out of trouble?"

"Yes, Mama."

She nodded, satisfied.

I don't remember exactly what we talked about after that. I remember laughing about something, sharing a moment of ease, as if we had all the time in the world.

I didn't know that a month later, she'd be gone. I didn't know that this was our last conversation. I didn't know that these words—words I had heard my entire life—would be the last things she ever said to me.

"God won't bless no mess."

"Find you a good woman and not be with a mud duck."

And then, I walked away.

The Phone Call That Changed Everything

It was just a regular day at work. The kind of day where you don't expect your entire world to shift in an instant.

The phone rang. I answered without thinking, expecting it to be something small, something I could brush off and return to my routine.

But the voice on the other end was different. My brother-in-law.

"She's gone."

For a second, I didn't understand.

"What?"

"She passed away."

The words slammed into me like a blow I hadn't seen coming. I felt like the air had been sucked from the room.

"No... No, no, no." My body locked up. My mind refused to process it.

She couldn't be gone. Not her. Not my mother.

I wanted to cry, but I couldn't. I wanted to scream, but I couldn't.

I was standing in the middle of my workplace, surrounded by people who had no idea that my entire world had just collapsed.

I hung up the phone and just stood there. Frozen. Lost. Not knowing what to do.

What do you do when the one person who always had the answers is no longer there?

The Funeral: Breaking Down, But Not Fully Grieving

The day of the funeral was a blur. I remember the church being filled with people. People who loved her. People who had been touched by her kindness, her wisdom, her unwavering strength.

I remember sitting in the front, staring at the casket, my chest so tight I could barely breathe.

I remember gripping the arms of the chair, trying to hold myself together.

Then the choir began to sing. Gospel music filled the air, and suddenly, everything crashed down on me.

I broke. The tears came hard and fast, years of love and loss and longing spilling out all at once. I sobbed. But even then, even in that raw moment, I still wasn't fully processing it. I was crying, yes, but I wasn't letting myself truly feel the weight of it. I was mourning, but I wasn't accepting. I was breaking, but I wasn't healing.

I left that funeral with a hole in my chest that I didn't know how to fill.

Years of Holding It In: Living with the Weight of Unspoken Grief

Grief is a strange thing. Sometimes, it comes all at once, hitting you like a storm. Other times, it sneaks up on you, little by little, settling into the corners of your soul, making itself at home without you even realizing it.

I thought I had moved on. I thought that crying at the funeral was enough. But the truth was, I had locked it away.

I kept living. I kept working. I kept moving. I didn't talk about her much. I didn't let myself go there.

Because if I did... If I actually allowed myself to sit with that question, to really think about it... The pain was unbearable. So I held it in. For years.

Until one night, it all came crashing down.

The Breakdown: "No Weapon Formed Against Me Shall Prosper"

I was in my 30s when it finally happened. It wasn't an anniversary. It wasn't her birthday. It was just another night.

I was sitting alone when a song came on.

"No weapon formed against me shall prosper."
Her favorite gospel song.

The second I heard it, something inside me shattered. I had heard this song a thousand times, but this time was different. This time, it took me back. Back to sitting in church next to her, watching her sway to the music, her hands lifted, eyes closed, fully believing in the words.

Back to being a little boy, hearing her whisper, *"You hear that, baby? No matter what happens, no weapon will prosper against you."* Back to every time she played it in the house, singing along as she cooked, as she cleaned, as she lived. And suddenly, I wasn't just listening to a song. I was with her again.

The weight of everything—every suppressed tear, every unspoken word, every moment I had pushed away—hit me all at once. And I broke. I sobbed. Not the quiet, controlled kind of crying. The deep, guttural, soul-crushing kind.

The kind that shakes your body, that makes you feel like you're drowning.

I cried for her. I cried for the years I had spent trying to pretend I was okay. I cried for every moment I had needed her and she wasn't there.

And for the first time since she left...

I finally let myself grieve.

The Healing: Finding Peace in the Pain

When the tears finally slowed, I felt lighter. Not because the pain was gone. The pain would never fully leave. But because I had let it out. I had finally given myself permission to feel. And in that moment, something else happened.

Forgiveness. For my biological mother. For the past. For myself.

Because I realized something—holding onto pain doesn't bring people back. But love? Love never leaves.

My stepmother's love was still with me. It was in the way I lived. It was in the way I loved my own children. It was in every lesson she ever taught me.

She was still here.

And she always would be.

Carrying Her Love Forward

THE IMPACT ON MY LIFE

Her Love Didn't Leave – It Lived On In Me

Grief changes, but love never leaves.

At first, I thought losing my stepmother meant losing her presence in my life completely. I thought that once she was gone, everything she had given me would slowly fade away. But I was wrong. Because the older I got, the more I realized... she never really left me. She was still there. In my choices. In my values. In the way I loved, the way I protected my family, the way I carried myself in the world.

She had spent my entire childhood pouring love into me, teaching me how to stand tall, how to walk with faith, how to build something strong for myself. And even though she was gone... she had left me with everything I needed to carry her love forward.

The Moment I Realized I Was Raising My Kids Like She Raised Me

It happened in a simple moment. One day, I was getting my kids ready to go somewhere.

I made sure they were dressed right—shoes clean, shirts tucked in, looking presentable.

And then, without even thinking, the words slipped out: "Ain't no child of mine walking around looking any kind of way."

The second I said it, I froze. Because that wasn't just my voice. That was her. That was her words, her standards, her love for me... coming out of my mouth.

I looked at my kids, and for a moment, I saw myself in them—the little boy she used to dress up, making sure I looked good before stepping out into the world. And right then, I felt her. She had raised me a certain way, and without even realizing it, I was passing that same love and care onto my own children.

It hit me like a wave. She was still here. Not just in my memories, but in the way I parented, the way I loved, the way I made sure my family was always taken care of.

She had raised me. And now, without even trying, I was raising my kids with the same love she
had given me.

Her Sayings Still Guide Me

It's funny how you don't realize how much
someone's words stick with you until you hear
yourself saying them.

My stepmother had a saying for everything.

"God won't bless no mess."

"Find you a good woman and not be with a mud
duck."

"Ain't nobody gonna raise my son but me."

She said these things so much that, as a kid,
I would roll my eyes. I would brush them off,

thinking they were just words. But they weren't just words. They were lessons. Lessons that have followed me into adulthood.

I've caught myself saying "God won't bless no mess" when making tough decisions, reminding myself that doing things the right way will always lead to better outcomes.

I've thought back to "Find you a good woman" every time I looked at my wife, knowing she would have approved, knowing she would have pulled me aside and said, "Now that's the kind of woman you build a life with."

And every time life tested me, every time I felt lost or unsure, I could hear her voice in the back of my mind.

"You stronger than you think, baby."

"No weapon formed against you shall prosper."

"You gon' be just fine."

Even now, she's still guiding me.

The Way I Love is Because of Her

Love wasn't just something my stepmother said—it was something she showed. She showed it in the way she took care of me. In the way she sacrificed for me. In the way she made sure I had everything I needed, even when it meant she went without.

She never had to say, "I love you."

I knew. Because love is action. Love is showing up. Love is protecting the people who mean the most to you. That's what she did for me. And now, it's how I love my own family. I love by showing up. By making sure my wife and kids know that I got them. By providing. By protecting. By making sure they never have to question if I'm in their corner. Everything I know about love, I learned from her.

Finding Strength in Her Memory

There have been moments in my life when I've felt completely lost. Moments when I didn't know what to do, when I felt like I was carrying the weight of the world on my shoulders. But in those moments, I always go back to her.

I think about how strong she was. How she handled everything life threw at her with grace and determination.

She never complained. She never broke down in front of me. She just handled it.

And when I feel like life is pushing me to my limits, I remind myself—she raised me to be strong.

She didn't just teach me how to survive. She taught me how to stand tall. She taught me how to face life head-on, no matter how hard it gets. And because of that, I know...

I can get through anything.

Signs That She's Still With Me

Even though she's gone, there have been moments where I felt her presence. Little things. Like hearing her favorite song at just the right time. Like seeing a certain color or smelling a certain perfume that reminds me of her.

Like waking up from a dream, feeling like she was just there, talking to me, reminding me she's still watching.

I don't know what happens after this life. I don't know if she can hear me. But I believe she's still here in some way. And I know that everything she taught me, everything she poured into me, still lives inside me.

She may not be physically here...

But her love will never leave me.

The Turning Point

ASKING THE QUESTION THAT CHANGED EVERYTHING

The Question That Lived Inside Me

Some questions stay with you, buried so deep inside that you almost forget they exist. But they don't disappear. They grow. They linger in the quiet moments, creeping into the spaces between your thoughts when you least expect them.

For years, I tried to ignore it. I told myself it didn't matter. That knowing the answer wouldn't change anything. That I had built a good life without knowing, so what was the point in asking now?

But I was lying to myself. Because no matter how much success I had found, no matter how much I had grown, no matter how much love I had surrounded myself with—that question never left me.

"Why did you leave me?"

It haunted me in ways I couldn't put into words. And one day, I realized... I couldn't carry it any longer.

I had to ask. I had to know.

The Fear of Asking

I had imagined the conversation a thousand times. In my mind, I had rehearsed every scenario, every possible response.

Maybe she would have a reason—something I had never thought of, something that would finally make sense of it all. Or maybe she would confirm my worst fears—that I wasn't wanted. That I was never enough. That she had walked away from me without looking back.

And that terrified me. Because once I asked... There would be no taking it back. The truth, whatever it was, would be real.

And I wasn't sure if I was ready for that.

The Day I Knew I Had to Do It

I don't know what made that particular day different. Maybe it was time. Maybe it was years of holding it in, pushing it down, pretending I didn't care. Or maybe it was my stepmother's voice in the back of my mind, pushing me forward.

"You strong, baby. You stronger than you think."

Whatever it was, something inside me shifted. And I knew—it was time. So I picked up the phone.

And I called her.

The Tension of the Call

The phone rang once. Twice. Three times.

My hands felt sweaty, my chest tight.

What if she didn't answer?

What if she did?

And then—

"Hello?"

Her voice was older than I remembered. Time had taken its toll, making it rougher, slower.

For a moment, I couldn't speak.

This was it. This was the moment.

The words felt heavy, stuck in my throat.

I almost hung up.

Almost convinced myself that this was a mistake.

But then, I took a deep breath. And I said it.

"Why did you leave me?"

The words came out softer than I had intended. But they carried years of pain. Years of confusion. Years of wondering. Years of needing to know.

And then—silence.

The Wait for an Answer

The silence stretched between us, long and unbearable.

I could hear my own heartbeat in my ears. I could hear her breathing on the other end of the line.

But she didn't speak.

Seconds passed, but it felt like an eternity.

Was she thinking?

Was she searching for an answer?

Or was she about to hang up, just like she had walked away all those years ago?

I clenched my jaw, bracing myself for whatever came next.

And then...

She finally spoke.

Life After the
Question

The Aftermath of Asking

When I hung up the phone, my hands were still shaking.

I had done it.

I had finally asked the question that had lived inside me for decades.

"Why did you leave me?"

But asking wasn't the hardest part.

The hardest part was everything that followed. Because once you ask a question like that...

You can't unhear the answer. You can't erase the truth.

And whether I was ready for it or not—my life had changed in that moment.

The Weight of Her Response

Her words echoed in my mind long after the call had ended.

Some of them made sense. Some of them didn't.

And some of them cut so deep that I wasn't sure if I would ever fully recover from them.

I replayed every detail, every pause, every hesitation.

Did she regret it?

Did she ever wonder about me?

Did she ever miss me?

Or had I spent my entire life grieving someone who had already moved on?

These questions gnawed at me in the weeks that followed.

I thought that asking her would bring me peace.

I thought that knowing the truth would make it easier to let go.

But instead...

It left me feeling more lost than ever.

Anger and Acceptance Battling Inside Me

There were days when I felt like I had made a mistake by asking.

Days when anger took over, filling the spaces where sadness had once lived.

How could she just walk away?

How could she live all these years without reaching out, without trying?

And how could I have spent so many years trying to be okay with it?

The anger burned hot, making me want to push the whole thing away again, pretend I never asked, pretend it didn't matter.

But the truth was—it *did* matter.

And no amount of anger was going to change that.

Because deep down, underneath the frustra-
tion and the pain, I knew I had done the right
thing.

I had needed to *ask*.

I had needed to *know*.

And now, I had to figure out what to do with
that knowledge.

The Impact on My Relationships

When you grow up with questions about love,
about abandonment, about whether or not you
were ever really wanted...

It affects how you love others.

It affects how you trust.

It affects how you build relationships.

For years, I had carried this silent fear with me—the fear of being left.

I didn't always recognize it. I didn't always see how it shaped the way I moved through life.

But it was there.

It was in the way I held onto people too tightly, afraid they would leave too.

It was in the way I sometimes kept people at a distance, protecting myself from the possibility of being hurt.

It was in the way I approached fatherhood, determined to never let my children feel what I had felt growing up.

And now, after finally confronting my past, I had to confront something else.

I had to decide how I wanted to move forward.

Because I refused to let her choices define me.

I refused to let her leaving be the thing that shaped the rest of my life.

I had built something different.

Something real.

Something strong.

And I wasn't going to let the past take that away from me.

Processing the Grief All Over Again

The thing about grief is—it doesn't follow a straight path.

Just when you think you've moved past it, just when you think you've healed, it comes back in waves.

And that's what happened to me.

Asking my mother why she left was supposed to bring me closure.

But instead, it opened up everything again.

I found myself thinking about my stepmother even more, missing her in a way that felt just as fresh as the day she died.

Because she was the one who stayed.

She was the one who never left.

She was the one who had filled the space my biological mother had left empty.

And now, as I tried to make sense of my past, I wished more than anything that she was still here.

To guide me.

To comfort me.

To tell me that no matter what happened, I was still her baby.

But she wasn't.

And for the first time in a long time...

I let myself grieve again.

Not just for my stepmother.

But for the little boy inside me who had been waiting for answers his whole life.

Finding Strength in My Own Story

One day, as I sat with all of these emo-tions—anger, grief, confusion—I had a realiza-tion.

I had spent so many years trying to make sense of my story.

Trying to understand why things happened the way they did.

Trying to find answers that, in the end, didn't really change the past.

But maybe...

Maybe my story wasn't about understanding *her*.

Maybe my story was about understanding *myself*.

Maybe it wasn't about why she left.

Maybe it was about what I did with the life I had been given.

Because I had built something out of the pain.

I had turned all the questions, all the abandonment, all the loss—into strength.

I had chosen *love*.

I had chosen *family*.

I had chosen to be better than the circumstances I was born into.

And at the end of the day, that was all the answer I needed.

I was not defined by who walked away.

I was defined by who stayed.

Carrying Both Truth and Forgiveness

It took me a long time to reach this place.

To hold both the truth of my past and the peace of my present in the same hand.

To accept that I may never fully understand my mother's choices.

To accept that I could still carry love for her, even if I didn't agree with what she had done.

To accept that forgiveness wasn't about saying it was okay.

It was about saying I refuse to let this pain control me anymore.

And so, little by little...

I let go.

Not of the love.

Not of the memories.

But of the weight.

Because I had spent too long carrying something that was never mine to hold.

A New Chapter Begins

After everything—the questions, the pain, the grief, the healing—I came to a simple realization.

My story was still being written.

And I had the power to decide what came next.

I wasn't that abandoned little boy anymore.

I was a man who had fought for his own happiness.

A man who had built a life that was worth living.

A man who had turned his pain into purpose.

And so, as I took a deep breath, standing on the other side of the hardest question I had ever asked...

I felt something I hadn't felt in a long time.

Peace.

Because for the first time in my life...

I was free.

Lessons from Loss

What Grief Taught Me

L oss is a teacher that never asks for permission to enter your life.

It shows up unannounced, rearranges everything you thought you knew, and forces you to sit with emotions you never wanted to feel.

For a long time, I thought grief was something I had to get over. That one day, I would wake up, and it wouldn't hurt anymore.

But I've learned something over the years—you don't get over loss. You learn how to carry it. You learn how to live with the empty spaces it leaves behind.

And if you're lucky...

You learn how to grow because of it.

Losing My Stepmother Changed Me Forever

When my stepmother died, something in me shifted.

I didn't just lose the woman who raised me.

I lost my anchor.

I lost the person who had always made me feel safe.

The person who had poured everything she had into making sure I never felt abandoned.

And when she was gone, I felt that familiar ache creeping back in—the one I had spent my whole life trying to silence.

"You stronger than you think, baby."

Her words played in my mind like a song on repeat.

She had spent my whole life preparing me for this moment—teaching me how to stand tall, how to move forward even when life tried to break me.

And now, it was time for me to live those lessons.

The Lessons She Left Behind

Even in her absence, my stepmother was still teaching me.

Her love had planted seeds in me that continued to grow, shaping the way I moved through the world.

I realized that everything she had done—every sacrifice, every lesson, every word of wisdom—had given me the tools to survive.

To love.

To lead.

To build a life that honored her.

And so, I started paying attention.

To the small ways she was still with me.

To the lessons she had left behind.

And this is what I learned:

Lesson 1: Love is an Action, Not Just a Word

My stepmother never had to say "I love you" for me to know it was true.

She showed it.

In the way she made sure I always had food on my plate.

In the way she worked extra hours so I could have the best clothes.

In the way she never left me, no matter how hard life got.

Love isn't just words.

Love is showing up.

And as I grew older, I made a promise to myself—

I would love the way she loved.

I would show up for my family.

I would make sure my wife and children never had to wonder if I loved them.

Because real love is undeniable.

It's in the actions.

Not just the words.

Lesson 2: Strength Doesn't Mean Hiding Your Pain

For years, I thought being strong meant never showing emotion.

Never crying.

Never breaking.

But my stepmother was the strongest person I ever knew.

And she felt everything.

She grieved. She cried. She prayed through her pain.

But she never let it stop her from moving forward.

She taught me that real strength isn't about pretending you're okay.

It's about acknowledging the pain—and choosing to keep going anyway.

Lesson 3: You Can't Carry Everything Alone

I spent so many years holding things in.

I didn't want to burden anyone with my pain.

I didn't want to talk about the things that hurt.

But my stepmother never carried her struggles alone.

She leaned on her faith.

She leaned on her family.

She believed that no one was meant to walk through life by themselves.

And as I grew older, I started to understand.

I started to let people in.

I started to let my wife see the parts of me that I had kept hidden for so long.

Because healing doesn't happen in isolation.

It happens in community.

Lesson 4: Forgiveness is for You, Not for Them

Forgiving my biological mother was one of the hardest things I've ever had to do.

For years, I held onto the pain of her absence.

I carried it like armor, convincing myself that if I never forgave her, I would never be hurt like that again.

But my stepmother always told me,

"Holding onto anger don't hurt nobody but you, baby."

At the time, I didn't want to hear it.

But she was right.

Forgiveness doesn't mean forgetting.

It doesn't mean excusing the pain someone caused you.

It means choosing to let go of the weight.

Choosing peace over resentment.

And when I finally forgave my mother...

I felt lighter than I ever had before.

Lesson 5: Your Story is Yours to Write

For a long time, I felt like my past defined me.

Like I would always be the boy who was left behind.

Like I would always be searching for something—or someone—to fill the empty spaces in me.

But my stepmother showed me that I was more than my circumstances.

She showed me that I had the power to write my own story.

And I did.

I built a life that was full of love.

I became the kind of father I had always wanted.

I made sure that my children would never have to question if they were wanted.

Because I was not just my past.

I was everything that came after it.

Her Legacy Lives in Me

Even though she's gone, my stepmother's love still shapes my life.

She taught me how to be a man.

She taught me how to love.

She taught me how to keep going, even when life feels impossible.

And now, it's my turn to pass those lessons down.

To my children.

To the people I love.

To anyone who needs to hear them.

Because her love didn't die with her.

It lives on.

In me.

In every choice I make.

In every person I love.

In every life I touch.

And I know...

That's exactly how she would have wanted it.

The True Meaning of Family

What Family Means to Me Now

G rowing up, I thought family was something simple.

It was the people you were born into, the ones you were tied to by blood.

But life has a way of teaching you lessons you never expected.

And one of the biggest lessons I've learned is this—

Family isn't just about blood.

Family is about who stays.

It's about who shows up.

It's about who chooses you—day after day, year after year, without conditions.

That lesson changed everything for me.

Because if family was only about blood, then why did the woman who gave birth to me leave?

And why did a woman who had no obligation to me—my stepmother—love me more than anything in this world?

The truth is, family is about love.

And the moment I let go of my expectations of what family should be...

I found something even greater than I could have imagined.

The Difference Between Family and Relatives

There's a difference between relatives and family.

Relatives are the people connected to you by DNA.

But family?

Family are the people who love you, protect you, and stand by you—even when they don't have to.

And that's what my stepmother did for me.

She didn't have to take me in.

She didn't have to pour her love into me.

She didn't have to give up everything to make sure I had a good life.

But she chose to.

She chose *me*.

And that's why she will always be my mother.

Because love is what makes a family—not just blood.

How My Definition of Family Changed Over Time

I used to believe that if someone was related to me, then they would always be in my life.

But I learned the hard way that blood doesn't guarantee loyalty.

I learned that some people who are supposed to love you...

Will leave.

And some people who have no obligation to you...

Will stand by you through everything.

That realization hurt at first.

It made me angry.

It made me question everything I had been taught about what family should be.

But over time, I started to understand.

Family isn't about who's supposed to love you.

It's about who actually does.

The Pain of Losing Family—Not Just in Death, But in Distance

Losing my stepmother was the hardest thing I ever experienced.

But there was another kind of loss that I didn't expect—

The loss of relationships with people who were still alive.

When she passed, things shifted in ways I never imagined.

People who were once close to me became distant.

Family members who had always been present began to drift away.

And it hurt—because I had already lost the most important person in my life.

I didn't think I would have to lose more.

But I did.

And I had to learn how to accept it.

Because sometimes, family is only family for a season.

And when that season ends, you have to be strong enough to let go.

Rebuilding My Own Definition of Family

For a long time, I struggled with what family meant after my stepmother passed.

But then I realized—I had the power to create my own definition.

I didn't have to hold on to relationships that no longer served me.

I didn't have to keep people in my life just because we shared the same DNA.

I could choose my family.

And so, that's what I did.

I surrounded myself with people who truly loved me.

I built a family based on love, loyalty, and mutual respect.

And most importantly, I made a promise to myself—

I would be the kind of parent my stepmother was to me.

A parent who showed up.

A parent who loved unconditionally.

A parent who chose family—not just by blood, but by action.

My Wife and Kids: The Family I Built

If there's one thing I'm proud of in this life, it's the family I built.

When I got married, I knew one thing for sure—

I wanted to create a home that felt safe, loving, and unbreakable.

I wanted my children to never question whether or not they were wanted.

I wanted my wife to always feel like she was loved the way she deserved.

Because I knew what it felt like to be abandoned.

And I refused to pass that pain down to the next generation.

So I became the kind of husband and father that I had always needed.

I loved fiercely.

I protected my family the way my stepmother protected me.

And I made sure that my children never had to wonder if their father would stay.

Because I will.

Always.

How My Stepmother's Love Lives On in My Own Family

There are moments when I catch myself saying something to my kids...

And I hear her voice.

"You better act like you got some sense."

"Ain't nobody gonna raise my son but me."

"God won't bless no mess."

I laugh every time it happens.

Because it reminds me that she's still here.

She's still with me.

Still shaping the way I parent, the way I love, the way I build my family.

Her legacy didn't end when she passed.

It continues—

Through me.

Through my children.

Through every lesson she ever taught me.

Letting Go of the Family That Didn't Choose Me

One of the hardest things I had to do was let go of the people who didn't show up for me.

For a long time, I held on.

I waited for them to change.

I waited for them to care.

I waited for them to prove that blood meant something.

But eventually, I had to accept the truth—

Some people will never be what you need them to be.

And that's okay.

Because I have enough.

I have the family I built.

I have the people who love me, not because they have to, but because they choose to.

And that's all that matters.

A Final Thought on Family

Family isn't perfect.

It's messy. It's complicated.

But the most important thing I've learned is this—

You have the power to define it.

You have the power to choose the people who pour into you, who uplift you, who stand beside you no matter what.

And once I stopped chasing love in the places it wasn't...

I found it in the places it had been all along.

Finding Peace

The Journey to Peace Wasn't Easy

For most of my life, I chased something I couldn't name.

I thought I was searching for answers.

I thought I was looking for closure.

I thought that if I could just understand why—why my biological mother left, why my stepmother had to go too soon, why certain people who were supposed to love me didn't—I would finally be free.

But the truth is, closure doesn't come from answers.

It comes from acceptance.

And peace?

Peace isn't something you find.

It's something you create.

And I had to learn how to create it for myself.

Letting Go of the Pain That Held Me Back

For years, I carried my pain like a badge of honor.

I thought holding on to it made me strong.

I thought keeping my walls up protected me from ever being hurt again.

But all it really did was weigh me down.

It kept me from trusting fully.

It kept me from loving freely.

It kept me from embracing the happiness that was right in front of me.

And one day, I realized—

I wasn't honoring my stepmother's love by holding on to pain.

I was dishonoring it.

Because she didn't raise me to live in bitterness.

She raised me to live.

To love.

To be happy.

And so, little by little...

I started letting go.

Forgiving My Biological Mother, Not for Her—But for Me

Forgiveness was never about making excuses for her.

It wasn't about pretending that her leaving didn't hurt me.

It wasn't about erasing the years of absence, the questions that haunted me, the pain that shaped me.

It was about freeing myself from the grip of the past.

Because as long as I held onto that resentment, I was still letting her control a part of me.

And I was tired of carrying that weight.

So I forgave.

Not because she asked for it.

Not because she deserved it.

But because I did.

Because I deserved peace.

Because I deserved to move forward without the past dragging me down.

Because I refused to let the choices of others define the rest of my life.

Accepting That Some Questions Will Never Have Answers

I spent so much time searching for an explanation that would make it all make sense.

I wanted there to be a reason.

I wanted something that would justify the pain.

But some questions?

They never get answers.

And the hardest lesson I had to learn was this—

You don't need an answer to heal.

Healing comes when you stop needing to understand the past...

And start focusing on building the future.

So instead of searching for answers, I made a decision.

I decided to write my own ending.

To take control of my own story.

To stop looking back and start moving forward.

How I Know She's Still With Me

Even though my stepmother is gone, I still feel her everywhere.

I feel her in the way I love my wife.

I feel her in the way I protect my children.

I feel her in the way I carry myself with strength, dignity, and purpose.

And every now and then, when I need her the most...

I hear her.

A whisper in the back of my mind.

"You gon' be just fine, baby."

"No weapon formed against you shall prosper."

"You stronger than you think."

And I know—

She never really left me.

She's been here all along.

Guiding me.

Loving me.

Watching over me.

And because of that...

I am never alone.

Choosing Love, Choosing Life

The past shaped me, but it does not define me.

The pain I went through made me stronger, but it does not control me.

I am more than what happened to me.

I am more than the people who left.

I am more than the hurt I once carried.

I am a father.

I am a husband.

I am a man who loves deeply and lives fully.

I am proof that love is stronger than pain.

That family is built, not just inherited.

That healing is possible, even when the wounds run deep.

And that peace...

Peace is something you create for yourself.

And I have finally found mine.

A Message to My Younger Self

I f I could go back in time and talk to the little boy I used to be, I would tell him this—

"You're gonna be okay."

"You are not what happened to you."

"You are loved. You are worthy. You are enough."

"And one day, you will build a life that is so full of love, so full of purpose, so full of joy... that the pain will no longer define you."

"And when that day comes... you will finally be free."

-Shamaine Cash

www.ingramcontent.com/pod-product-compliance
Lightning Source LLC
Chambersburg PA
CBHW061657120626
46550CB00003B/982